cerebus syndrome

frisk arnold

Presentation by *BookLeaf Publishing*

Web: www.bookleafpub.com

E-mail: info@bookleafpub.com

ISBN: 9789357214179

First edition 2023

to phoenix starr & bunny ikari, thank you for being the voice that i didn't have. this is a healing process that's gained so much traction and movement since you both came into my life, and shared clarity with me. you help me move towards full closure everyday, and you don't realize it.

and to andrew downing, teya milan, kacey muerer, and phoenix starr, you four have seen the inner workings of me and still have love for me in your heart. if there's soulmates in this world, you guys are mine. you changed me in the way i see the world in a positive way & gave me so much hope in humanity. polaroids of you four never leave the wallet i carry around daily. i like to think you four are the reminder to keep going.

and to all my friends and family, thank you for always encouraging me and being that push in my life. i love you all.

ACKNOWLEDGEMENT

to nicolas navarro, thank you for making the front cover of this book. i appreciate you for bringing this book to life.

PREFACE

just a reminder that this poetry book serves a purpose - not to destroy, but to rebuild what was lost. this book features themes that may be unsuitable for children and adolescents (18+) for graphic topics that may be triggering to the reader. themes such as SA, abuse, blood, death, and suicide may be present in these pages. please do heed caution and be aware of the content before proceeding for your own well being.

if you believe you are in a domestic violence situation, please call the domestic violence hotline at 800-799-7233 or text START to 88788.

if you believe you are a danger to yourself and have suicidal thoughts/ideations, please call the crisis help hotline at 988 or text HOME to 741741.

to my parents who i know will read this, i do apologize for the content.

dissection

he breaks though my translucent skin
using the scalpel i trusted him with
hoping to find a garden that awaits him
flush with flowers, dewy from rain
but that was the past body,
and this is the present body
enveloped in mental disorders
and phobias - an inhospitable place
like constantly going through
winter weather in antartica
he combs through gangrene buildup,
blowflies instead of butterflies,
body horrors - a shock website sight -
constructing tumors in my organs,
warning signs developing rapidly
as the parasites make me their host,
and i still feel that scalpel. my body
remembers those details. my brain
does not. jesus did not die a
martyr. he died a fool.

shibari

the trauma hive brain memory block
presents itself as shibari bondage -
your body is locked into a vegetated
state, albeit familiar. the ropes feel
like grape vineyards wrapping around
the torso, anchoring the wrists and
ankles into submission. ignorance
is bliss when innocence is lost.

the lesions left behind from the
friction of the constraints hides
under a jungle of vines. unwrapping
the dressings & discovering what
lies underneath is the most pragmatic
solution, but self-preservation for
myself became more important.

autumn

leaves fall, and so do secrets eventually.
fruits fall from the tree once ripened,
and we fall for the wrong people,
consistently repeating behaviors
like revolving doors. when you're wearing
rose-colored glasses, the red flags just look
like flags. it's easier to forget about the upcoming
blistering winter, than to let this mask fall
like autumn leaves in inclement weather.

if the forest is home, i am homesick for
a home i haven't fully discovered yet.

hikkiomori

our frequencies collided like a car crash,
left me with whiplash, quickly oscillating
into violent crescendos of white noise,
you left me without a voice. like cain,
sin crouched at the door, and you opened
pandora's box. white lies augmented into
memories - shattered into hundreds of
pieces. to be complicit with silence,
to be accustomed to denying the truth,
is a learned niche. the death of self
is something i will always lament.

to open the box and explore those sins
comes a grim curiosity that can kill a cat.

blanket treatment

the same sheets you used to get
tangled in with me at night began
to feel like insulation shredding
my skin, like lint balls opting
to substitute for the razors.
symptoms of anger become
physical. sleep is a foreign
language. sleep is a phenomenon
virtually unknown to me.

when i was still soft cotton,
when i was still heavy blanket,
when i was still warm fleece
embracing you in comfort,
you treated me like sandpaper
against leather upholstery.

once, i was heaven sent,
however you were hellbent on
ensuring my reservation within
your death note. i hope the lint
in your blankets from where i
used to lay irritates your skin.

stigmata

with the first nail embedded into your right
palm, the same one that held so tightly
onto mine and held onto the past within
a hiker's backpack weighing heavy on
your shoulders, i nailed you to the cross.

you began believing in you becoming
something like a god, more powerful
than anyone in your previous family lineage.

the second nail came through your left
palm. after i left, you painted the blood
i shed for you onto them, and their identity
was fragmented into segments. like a rock,
you were sedentary at the time.

with the third nail, forcing it's way through
tissue and bone, it went through your
right foot. they say a rabbit's foot is
lucky, but the rabbit approached the
dinner table to an empty platter and
a very hungry wolf holding a steak
knife, salivating at the taste of their
prey, and soon-to-be dinner.

with the fourth nail, you were damned
to the plywood planks as the last person
familiar with your previous malevolent
actions, but choosing to forgive & forget,
was brandished in scars from you.
blood soaked into the wood, into the
dirt below that you would soon find
yourself in, into the sheets we laid in,
i still am finding blood on my bedsheets
from the blood you keep spilling. you
don't feel complete getting even, but i do.

hibiscus

vigilance means nothing when vengeance
means everything to you. in your verses are
vices, using tactical psychological warfare
to groom and take advantage of future prey
vermillion hibiscus flowers paint the black
and white walls of bedrooms i haven't seen
and may never see. there's no mistake,
like a shark, i smell the bloodshed.

when you begin to empathize with the
monster, you begin to see it in the mirror.

one day, he will be pulling petals off
of the hibiscus flowers like tearing wings
off of butterflies, reciting this like prayer:
forget me,
forget me not,
forget me,
forget me not,
the last petal prevents him from forgetting
about the warzone i trampled through to
satiate his unhealed childhood wounds.

three of swords

sword one:
the truth appeared as distorted polaroids
left out in the sun. the truth appeared as
a cacophony of noise. the upbringing in
a flawed ecosystem blighted facts from
fiction. the plea bargain was not guilty,
but it was me who saw the bloodstains
on his hands that night. closure became
fantasy because he handed me the sword,
led others to believe fictional tough claims.

sword two:
the typewriter served pages full of minor
discrepancies, which would be served
later on as major deviations from the
original plot. they're the weather man,
i know you won't believe it, but isn't it
funny that you ain't seen the sun in weeks?

sword three:
once he removed the rabbit
mask from his features,
carefully placed to present
himself as a fragile human,
he revealed himself to be the

predator with fresh flesh stuck
between his teeth, ready to draw
more blood. it was dominating the
food chain, or removing the problem
entirely. as the story is told, we all
retaliated, subdued, and ripped the
mask off revealing the animosity
behind those words & actions.

7.9.1958

an eight point three magnitude tsunami
plunges into the gulf of alaska like mother
nature is on a path of destruction,
like how the genesis flood narrative
sent forth noah to build an arc to survive
the chaos of the great flood to rebuild
the earth into perfect symmetry.

the question remains: who have i been
praying to all this time? the distress
signals aren't reaching whoever is
on the other line, and five innocent
lives got whisked away by the waves.

would i have believed in god if he
helped bring all five lives to safety?
or would the aftermath still linger?

perspectives

i was trapped in a mirror maze, approaching
the glass from different angles, watching my
body morph into different shapes and sizes.
it was there that the thought disturbed me:
what point of view am i seeing in? is it my
own or his? did he see something different
as i approached the glass, or did we see
the same grotesque thing staring back at
us in the mirror? if there's a looking glass,
i'd like to see through my perspective.
not through his.

venus fly trap

as a venus fly trap, you captured things
like mosquitos and hearts. yet still
we are lines that are perpendicular,
we met once and did not meet again.

how tragic it was to be a victim of a
wolf when i was the rabbit awaiting trial
jury pressed for a sentencing.
premonition brings on the idea of
a withering field,
a slow burn summer,
a miserable drought,
a forest fire of fury retaliating against
me, developing a court case i can't win.
there was no bargaining, there was only
a verdict: guilty as charged.

flora/fauna

when did the bustling streets of
flora and fauna clustered
haphazardly in the earth die out
and the monotonous gray slabs
of concrete replace that? when
did the wildlife become irrevocably
conditioned to be territorial creatures,
claiming untouched land that we have
not set foot through yet? did it happen
overnight? if i could get that lush
landscape back, would i be happy
where i ended up, or would the weeds
take over my bones once more?

siren's song

singing sweetly to a chorus of church hymns,
i always get lost in the wonders of the ocean
wandering down to the great depths and back
to the surface to share my voice with the world.

his eyes become glazed with feeling, unable to
differentiate between love and lust, and
suddenly,
i am luring him down to the bottom of the ocean
never to be seen again. ursula, take my voice so
i don't pass this curse onto other vulnerable
sailors.

reciprocal altruism

falling into the rabbit hole of false
sincerity, benevolence would win
over in the face of repeated
malevolence. like alice, i drank
from the bottle and shrank down
smaller than a toad. this resistance
to my benevolence has become
bigger than me. growing up,
unlearning habits, becoming what
ever i was pre-war left me with
permanent scars, mostly unseen.

i keep hoping this is a dream, but i keep
waking up sicker than i was yesterday,
wanting to stay in my deep slumber.

purification process

my job was to purify the world,
full of specters and creatures
grotesque in appearance. it was
my duty to stabilize the rocky
ambience and translate the
cuneiform inscriptions scratched
into the walls to perhaps understand
how to get these tough claims into a
choke hold instead of the alternate:
writing. once walls full of color,
now became a black and white slate
devoid of color & light.

loving you - i realized - shouldn't
have been a purification process.

once you held the sun in your hands,
shining through and around my body.
but you left me with the moon, surrounded
by the very specters i desired to purify.

operant conditioning

negative reinforcements became the blueprints
that i navigated and refined my environment
and my behavior. like a ghost forever left to
haunt the halls, waiting for the next séance,
misery and atrophy was the ball and chain
preventing me from finding closure.

the reward i was promised at the end of
the maze is something i'm convinced
never fucking existed in the first place.

unlearning what i was taught
taught me to keep my heart shut
because you can't break something
that can't be opened.

sober

the smoke and smog from the palo santo
overwhelmed the headfog from the merlot,
from the stockholm syndrome that persisted
with years, counteracting chances of recovery
salt, peppercorns, sage, rosemary, and mint
decorated the altar as the candles were lit,
the candles with our initials carved into it,
beginning to burn vehemently as i imagined
that red glowing string connecting us two

in your bedroom as a ghost, i could only see
you on a drug binge. i could only feel sorry
as i held the knife - the same one that you
said i used on you - in my hands. it wasn't
meant for you. it was never meant for you.
i cut our cord,
and watched me burn out faster than you.
watching myself disconnect from you
became one of the most sobering
moments i've ever encountered.

querces robur

i think about all the insurmountable times i have
watched myself shave off the bark of my skin
to watch others thrive and blossom violently like
wildflowers and chrysanthemums. i think of how
you have always been a tree – tall, mighty,
powerful
- with roots that don't seem to make mine feel
like
weeds. teach me, for i aspire to be luminous,
tree.

i dream of worlds made of jasmine and
honeysuckle,
of utopias devoid of the bark i've shaved off my
back.

i dream of sap that feels a little less like magma
and
a lot more like maple syrup. i dream of roots that
doesn't feel like granite and completely calcified.
teach me, for i aspire to be luminous, tree.

genesis

creating something in my own image
something so powerful that it birthed
something that mattered. with the
birth of chaos, the paper was the
bread and the ink was my wine.

the serpents had a hand in character
development, but i'd bring a ravenous
storm of locusts before i agreed to
becoming everything that i hated.

i'd accept what mattered, and bring
everything that mattered to life.

luminary

the glowing light bulb pigments the
room in a vivarium of colors, exploding
through the washed-out pallet of
monochrome into everything all at once.
the light is divine incarnate; reckless
& relentless. i see her appearing in
different illuminations, only burning
bright like flares when her eyes find mine.

in this world's atrium filled with heaven's
lights, you are the paragon of euphoria.
illuminate me in all your shades and
shadows, and radiate your sunlight
through me. childhood escapism
through light - burning bright.